SHADOW LANGUAGE

For Emrah

Kelly Stuart

SHADOW LANGUAGE

OBERON BOOKS
LONDON

First published in 2008 by Oberon Books Ltd
521 Caledonian Road, London N7 9RH
Tel: 020 7607 3637 / Fax: 020 7607 3629
e-mail: info@oberonbooks.com
www.oberonbooks.com

A catalogue record for this book is available from the British Library.

ISBN: 978-1-84002-842-3

Cover design by Dan Steward

Characters

	In the Puppet Show:
JUNE	
TRACEE	HACIVAT
LITTLE GIRL	KARAGÖZ
ORHAN	DONKEY
WAITER	WOLF
GABE	LITTLE GIRL PUPPET
WOMAN	KOOLIOZ
CHILD	MINISTER
BAWER	MOON
MURAT	TWO-HEADED COP
TURKISH GENERAL	AMERICAN PRESIDENT
SOSIN	JUNE PUPPET
CEM	CEM PUPPET

The shadow puppetry in this play is based on the Ottoman "Karagöz" shadow puppet tradition, which uses puppets pressed up against a screen. The actor playing CEM should perform HACIVAT and KARAGÖZ, while other actors can perform the voices and puppets of other characters. A sense of playfulness and even a bit of improvisation is encouraged.

Shadow Language was first performed on 20 February 2008 at Theatre503, London, with the following cast:

JUNE, Beverley Longhurst

TRACEE, Miranda Foster

ORHAN, Hemi Yeroham

WOMAN / SOSIN, Zina Badran

MURAT / CEM, Khalid Laith

BAWER, George Georgiou

GABRIEL, Eugene Washington

LITTLE GIRL / CHILD, Nancy Wallinger

All other parts played by members of the company.

Director Tim Stark

Designer Cordelia Chisholm

Lighting Designer Mark Doubleday

Sound Designer Duncan Chave

Shadow Puppets designed & animated by
      Chiara Ambrosio & Xristina Penna

Prologue

In dark: drums. Lights up. A Shadow Puppet Show:

HACIVAT: To the eye of the ignorant—

KARAGÖZ appears from hiding.

KARAGÖZ: That's him.

HACIVAT tries to strike him. KARAGÖZ disappears. HACIVAT regains his composure.

HACIVAT: —This light produces just images, shadows...a likeness of the world.

KARAGÖZ appears behind HACIVAT.

Behold the meanings that are hidden in this show!

KARAGÖZ kicks HACIVAT in the ass.

Ow. Fiend. Hardheaded vulgarian.

KARAGÖZ: Every night you follow me and you talk! You talk talk talk talk.

HACIVAT: My speech is an art.

KARAGÖZ: The sound of a pig making fart after fart.

HACIVAT hits KARAGÖZ, KARAGÖZ kisses HACIVAT.

HACIVAT: That is not an orifice!

They fight—but quickly get tired. Exhausted they try to whack each other but their limbs move in slow motion. Stalemate. Both have stopped. KARAGÖZ tries one more blow but can't lift his arm to strike...

(*Out of breath.*) Violence gets you nowhere.

KARAGÖZ: If we were in the village...

HACIVAT: What?

KARAGÖZ: If we were back in the village...

HACIVAT: Village? What village.

KARAGÖZ: I'd steal all your sheep and make a big sacrifice.

Eyes appear everywhere. Wolves' eyes. HACIVAT and KARAGÖZ KARAGÖZ tremble while trying to maintain their composure.

HACIVAT: (*Loud and false:*) I do not come from a village. Do you?

KARAGÖZ: Of course I don't drink swillage. Why?

HACIVAT: No, I said village.

KARAGÖZ: We heard you. Enough. Nobody wants your swillage.

The DONKEY enters, kisses and licks KARAGÖZ.

Our old donkey still thinks that he knows us.

To the DONKEY.

Get out of here!

The DONKEY persists.

Get lost. I've never seen you before. Cut it out! Stop it!

HACIVAT: Obviously, this beast has got us confused with somebody else.

The DONKEY licks them both.

KARAGÖZ: Kero here!!! Derkev...Ço!Ço! Ço Ço!

HACIVAT: (*To the audience.*) As I was saying: Behold the hidden meanings of these images...

The DONKEY is obscenely licking KARAGÖZ everywhere.

KARAGÖZ: Bese! Makuro—Tu duxazi ez mejiyate berdim ser çavete. Ez di hestiye bave tenim aa!!! Here!
(**Boy, I will put your brain on top of your eyes... I will fuck your father's bones. Go!**)

8

HACIVAT: Because when the candle goes out, the pictured persons cease to exist.

KARAGÖZ: What?

Blackout.

Act One

Istanbul. A tea house. JUNE and TRACEE sit opposite each other. A LITTLE GIRL appears, places a scale on the ground in front of JUNE.

LITTLE GIRL: Buyurun! Buyurun!

JUNE: What does she want?

TRACEE: She wants to weigh you.

LITTLE GIRL: Çok iyi, beş milyon!

TRACEE: If you pay her, twenty more kids are going to come.
Have you got enough for everyone?

JUNE: I don't want to attract a crowd.

TRACEE: No, they won't like it.

JUNE: Who?

LITTLE GIRL: Beş milyon. Çok iyi.

JUNE: No thank you.

TRACEE: Hayir.

LITTLE GIRL: Buyrun.

JUNE: *(Imitates TRACEE sternly.)* Hayir. HAYIR.

The LITTLE GIRL moves away.

TRACEE: You have to be ruthless with children here.
I just came from Hasankeyf.
I was there to sketch the ruins.
Just outside a cave
A hundred children
came out of nowhere like bats
nearly tore me to shreds.
This old Moslem man
came to my rescue

and chased them away
But I had to keep peeling
his hands off my body
I finally managed to ditch him in the mosque
I was at a loss
because my Turkish is weak.
We are naked
when we don't speak the language.
We are just there,
our expressions betray us.
We're standing there with no way to lie
And that's when opportunists strike.

Pause.

What brings you to Istanbul?
Here on vacation?

JUNE: I'm here with a friend.

TRACEE: Oh? Where is he?

JUNE: At the—hotel.

TRACEE: Which hotel?

JUNE: I'm not sure. He's coming back. Soon.

TRACEE: He left you alone here with that suitcase?

JUNE: Yes. That's why he's coming back.
    He didn't want me to carry it.
    He takes care of everything.

TRACEE: Why didn't he just carry it then?

JUNE: Because he had a big bag of his own.
    A big bag. We have a lot of luggage.

TRACEE: Are you here for a while, or did you just over-pack?

JUNE: You ask a lot of questions.

TRACEE: I'm American. That's how we are.

You can't get a straight answer out of the Turks.
You ask anyone a question,
there are fifteen different answers.
Depending on who
they think is listening.
Depending on what
they think you want to hear.
Depending on what
they think could earn them a profit
or make them look good
Or make them feel safe.
It's not like Americans who are sincere
And say what we think.
Has someone abandoned you?

JUNE: What makes you think that?

TRACEE: I've watched you sit alone here for hours, just you
and your luggage.

JUNE: Why?

TRACEE: I'm an artist, I wanted to draw you. You have a nice
bone structure dear, see? But you shouldn't sit here alone.

JUNE: God is with me.

TRACEE: Okay.
You're not one of those missionaries are you?
You didn't come to convert people, did you?
Three missionaries in Maltya, just got their throats cut.
This isn't Texas, you have to be careful.

JUNE: I'm not from Texas.

TRACEE: Where are you from?
Are you here doing the whole
seven churches of Anatolia thing?
Did you come here to see the Aya Sophia?

JUNE: What's that?

TRACEE: The Hagia Sophia...church of Divine Wisdom?

JUNE: Never heard of it.

TRACEE: I can give you a tour.
It's right over there.
Built by Justinian 460 AD.
For a pilgrim, you are strikingly ignorant—

JUNE: I'm not interested in that.

TRACEE: What?

JUNE: I'm waiting for a message.

TRACEE: From your friend?

JUNE: Yes.

TRACEE: What kind of friend?
Someone you traveled with?
American... Turkish?

JUNE: He was born here. I knew him from America. He
said...he might be leaving and then...

TRACEE: He disappeared.

JUNE: Yes.

TRACEE: Did you help him? Did you give him all of your
money?

JUNE: No. We didn't think there was a problem,
but after I realized...
My church sent me to help him.
My church would have given him money
if they'd understood...

TRACEE: What?

JUNE: He was having some problems with people.
He told us he might have to come back...
And then he was gone.

13

TRACEE: Does he want you to find him or he's hiding
from you?

JUNE: I was sent here to save him.

TRACEE: What… His soul?

JUNE: No.

TRACEE: His body? If he wants you to save him, why doesn't
he call you? Why doesn't he tell you where you
should go?

JUNE: Maybe he can't.

TRACEE: Why not?

JUNE: That's something I came to find out.

TRACEE: But how are you going to do that?

JUNE: I know the name of the place that he's from.
He told me all about his family.
It's like I know them.

TRACEE: Where's he from?

JUNE: It's…a place called Dersim. It has another name, a
Turkish name but the real name is Dersim.

TRACEE: That's Kur——K. Something K.

JUNE: K?

TRACEE: Shh.

JUNE: Do you mean—Kurdish?

TRACEE: Yes.

JUNE: Do you speak Kurdish?

TRACEE: I have a Kurdish lover. Had.
I left my husband in LA
for Murat.
Well, first there was Wolfgang.
That was in Germany and France

After Wolfgang,
I had a chance to come home
But I had already fallen for Murat
So I got a divorce
And got half the money
And came back here
And now I have nothing.
Murat took it all
And now he's gone.
I had a Kurdish lover. He's gone.

JUNE: I don't know what to say.

TRACEE: Don't sleep with any of these guys here,
These carpet dealers
All of them are gigolos.

JUNE: Okay.

TRACEE: The K word. The K.
And even as I say it
I know I should be more discreet.
I say Tracee, haven't you learned from your mistakes?
After five years, you'd think I'd know better.
The Turks will say there are no Kurds
But I said to my boss, I said, Mehmet Bay
There certainly ARE such people
I have seen them.
In fact, the only men I want to sleep with are Kurdish,
so if you want to tell me these people don't exist, then I'd
like to know who I've been fucking all this time.
And at that point he told me my work visa had be denied
and they would no longer be able to pay me. And at that
moment I had the sudden realization that maybe I am
just WAY TOO HONEST.

JUNE: Do you need money?

TRACEE: When people commit suicide here, they jump from tall bridges or minarets.

JUNE: That's not what happened to Cem.

TRACEE: Murat is the same, thank God he got away.

JUNE: Was he fleeing the government?

TRACEE: No. His whole family. But if he was here we could take you to Dersim. If we can find him...

JUNE: Do you know someone else who can tell me how to get Dersim? I haven't got time. I need to go now. I need to find him now. Do you know someone?

Lights out.

Shadow Puppets:

KARAGÖZ, HACIVAT, *the* DONKEY. *Off-growling is heard from the* WOLF. WOLF'*s shadow grows and falls over* KARAGÖZ. *Growling.*

KARAGÖZ: What does he want?

HACIVAT: He says you are under arrest.

KARAGÖZ: For what?

The WOLF *growls again.*

HACIVAT: For speaking in—some other language.

KARAGÖZ: What language was that?

HACIVAT: Oh great Efendim, what language was he speaking?

The WOLF *growls again.*

You were speaking a language that doesn't exist.

KARAGÖZ: Huh?

The WOLF *growls again.*

HACIVAT: Maybe the Judge can explain.

The WOLF *disappears / reappears with a Judge's robe. It growls again.*

(*Interpreting the growl.*) You speak in a language divisive to our state.

KARAGÖZ: But sir, I was only just talking to my donkey.

The WOLF *growls:*

HACIVAT: (*Interprets:*) The speech of divisive language is forbidden. We are Turks.

KARAGÖZ: (*Secretly to* HACIVAT.) We are?

HACIVAT: Yes We're Turks. Turks.

KARAGÖZ: Turks!...

HACIVAT: (*Interpreting the growls.*) We must speak TURKISH.

KARAGÖZ: But sir, my donkey doesn't speak Turkish.

The WOLF *growls:*

HACIVAT: Then have this donkey taken out and shot!

KARAGÖZ: No!

KARAGÖZ tries to run. The WOLF *opens its mouth wider and wider to swallow them all. Everything goes to black.*

Istanbul carpet shop: in dim light a flashlight illuminates red woven carpets hanging from the ceiling and walls. ORHAN, TRACEE and JUNE. JUNE clings to her suitcase.

ORHAN: I am not a terrorist.

TRACEE: She knows you're not a terrorist Orhan.

ORHAN: I'm Kurdish, yes, I'm not the PKK.

JUNE: (*Whispers.*) Do you speak Kurdish?

ORHAN: I can do business in eight languages.
   But that was my first.
   I spoke nothing else
   until I was eight.
   Then we came to Istanbul.

   ORHAN shines a light on the carpets.

   If the power hadn't gone out
   You could see the deep color in these
   The girl who makes this goes color blind when she's done

TRACEE: She's not here to buy a carpet.

ORHAN: We have Kilims. Something smaller. We take credit cards.

JUNE: No.

TRACEE: I didn't bring her to buy a carpet.

ORHAN: We can ship to your home address.

JUNE: I really didn't come all this way for a—

ORHAN: I can always hold it for you, if you like something you can put down deposit.

TRACEE: Dinlebe! She's not here to buy a carpet. You people don't listen. That's the problem with this country. Everything has to be said three times. She didn't come here for a carpet. Didn't COME HERE FOR A CARPET.

ORHAN: Forgive me.

JUNE: I'm looking for someone.

ORHAN: You've found him.

JUNE: No, a friend of mine who is missing.

ORHAN: Tamam. Okay. I am detective as well.

JUNE: (*Whispers.*) He's Kurdish.

ORHAN: Why are you whispering?

JUNE: Isn't it illegal?

ORHAN: No. No. Things are much better now.
We can speak our language.
We can listen to our music.
We're getting our rights.

TRACEE: But you wouldn't say that to the police or the Jandarma.

ORHAN: Things are much better now.

TRACEE: They could still kill you.

ORHAN: I think people are tired of killing. If you're just doing business, why should they kill? So I'm Kurdish, so what. Why kill me for that?

JUNE: Of course nobody should kill you for that but they do, don't they? That's what my friend said. If you say that you're Turkish, then everything's fine. If you say that you're Kurdish...

ORHAN: I don't have to announce it.

JUNE: My friend said he couldn't live like that.

ORHAN: And this is the friend you're looking for?

JUNE: Yes.

ORHAN: And how do you know him? From here?

JUNE: From America.

ORHAN: Kurdish.

JUNE: Yes.

ORHAN: He is your lover?

JUNE: No. I knew him from church.

ORHAN: He is Christian Kurd?

JUNE: You think that's funny?

ORHAN: Yes. Christians are funny. I could sell these people anything. Who else would believe in a virgin birth?

TRACEE: Who believes 70 sex starved virgins are waiting for them to get into heaven?

ORHAN: Not me.

JUNE: You think it's funny I've come all this way to help someone. So that's funny to you. You think it's funny that someone is good, a good man, who never hurt anyone is in trouble? Should I forget about him? Because Christians don't forget those in need. If someone needs us we're there, no matter what. And no he wasn't my lover, my boyfriend. It was nothing like that. He was pure, and people get jealous, so they gossip and attack and make up false stories. But he would never strike back. He's not the kind of person who would hurt anyone ever. Even if somebody let him down... I know he'd forgive them. Even towards the people who hurt him a lot...even to people who maybe sent him away...and that's why I... I told you I'm a Christian. Our church...gave... When he came... We helped him resettle...

ORHAN: Resettle from where?

JUNE: From here. From—he said, he wouldn't say the word Turkey. He said he came from Kurdistan.

ORHAN: Okay, don't say that. I hope for it yes, but that word is dangerous.

JUNE: What's wrong.

ORHAN: It will get you in trouble.

JUNE: But that's where he said he was from.

ORHAN: He wasn't talking about Iraq.

JUNE: No. He's from a village near Dersim.

ORHAN: Okay, Lady, you don't want to find him.

JUNE: Yes I do.

ORHAN: I'm saying you don't. Forget it.

JUNE: Why? What's wrong? Don't you know where Dersim is?

ORHAN: Of course I know.

JUNE: 'Cause it's not on the map.

ORHAN: What's the name of this friend?

JUNE: Cem Yildiz. He's from the Kureyşan Aşiret. In Dersim.

ORHAN: Kureyşan.

JUNE: You've heard of it?

ORHAN: Of course. I'm Kureyşan as well. There's a lot of us.

JUNE: And you know where Dersim is.

ORHAN: Lady, there are thirty million Kurds in this world.

JUNE: But I'm only looking for Cem, and he's—

ORHAN: How did he disappear?

JUNE: Homeland Security.

ORHAN: What's that?

TRACEE: Like Jandarma.

ORHAN: They have Jandarma in America?

TRACEE: Where was he taken?

JUNE: I don't know.

ORHAN: Why? Why would they take him?

JUNE: It doesn't make sense. He lived all those years, he
was good.
But everything has changed in my country.

TRACEE: Yeah, gone to shit.

JUNE: No, it's... I think America is good,
we have good intentions.
I'm sorry, but we do.
Here I am, trying to help.

ORHAN: Why? What is your business in this?

JUNE: My church. I'm Christian. We knew him.
They pooled their money to send me here.
We just want to help...
find out where he is.
Nobody can get information.
I know he has a sister here.
If you help me, I can help you,
he taught me things, from his language.
Things I can remember, names of places.
Once we get to Dersim...

ORHAN: (*In Zaza.*) Tu zonê Zazaki qiseykena?
(*You understand Zazaki?*)

JUNE: Na ez nizanim. Ez Kurmanci dı zanim.
(*No, I speak Kurmanci.*)

ORHAN: Savaşçıların tarafında mı bu?
(*Is she with the guerrillas?*)

TRACEE: Tabii ki değil. (*Of course not.*)

ORHAN: Ne biliyor o zaman? (*Then what does she know?*)

TRACEE: Çok parası var. Murat'ı bulmama yardım et, sana
herşeyi anlatayım.
(*She's got money. I'll tell you, if you help me find Murat.*)

ORHAN: Yeni kızarkadaşıyla Diyarbakır'a gitti. Unut onu.
Beni al.
(*He went to Diyarbekir, with his new girlfriend. Forget him.
You can have me.*)

TRACEE: Ne yeni kızarkadaşı be? Kimmiş bu kız? Kim?
(*What new girlfriend? Who is she? Who?*)

JUNE: What are you saying?

ORHAN: Dersim can mean a lot of things.

JUNE: You can take me there.

ORHAN: I don't want to get involved with bad things.
Things are better, much better for us now,
The war is over, ten years ago, yes
Ten years ago, things were really bad, but right now
It's better to leave things alone.
Look, I have beautiful, beautiful Kilims... Kurdish
Kilims.

JUNE: Sorry. I don't. If you can't... I just have to find him.

ORHAN: Why?

TRACEE: Stop being an idiot Orhan.

ORHAN: Listen, this country, it's a beautiful country. We don't
have a threat to our lives now. If he was involved when
things were bad, back then. Well, You just want to keep
away from that.

JUNE: Please, can you just take me to Dersim? Is it far? I can
pay you. My church has given me money for this.

ORHAN: Dersim is full of PKK. Is that who you're looking
for?

JUNE: No.

ORHAN: I think so.

JUNE: No. It's just where Cem's family is from.

ORHAN: He spoke Zaza or Kurmanci?

JUNE: He spoke both. His family spoke both.

ORHAN: Because most people from Dersim, speak Zaza not Kurmanci.
I think he was keeping some secrets from you.

JUNE: No.

ORHAN: He wasn't from Dersim, he was with the guerillas. If he spoke Kurmanci that means he CAME to Dersim. Probably from Diyarbekir.

JUNE: No, it wasn't like that. His father came from Kiği, his father spoke Kurmanci. His mother spoke Zazaki. He was born in Dersim. He told me everything...

ORHAN: Everything except where it is.

JUNE: A hundred thousand Kurdish people were killed there. In 1938.

ORHAN: Okay. Shhh. You want to go to Dersim to help someone, it sounds like you're helping the PKK. There's no way I'm getting involved with that.

JUNE: My church gave me money for this.

TRACEE: What kind of church...?

ORHAN: How much?

JUNE: Enough to pay someone very very well for his help. Maybe you're not the right person.

ORHAN: And what are you going to do when you get there? How will you find him.

JUNE: There's a place he told me I have to see. He said, if you can see it, you'll understand everything. He said these words, "Caven te cixas xwesin."
(*In Kurdish: **How beautiful are your eyes.***)

ORHAN: Do you know what that means?

JUNE: I think I'll find him there, in that place, or someone who can tell me where he is.

ORHAN: That's not a place. What he said to you, is that you have to see how beautiful your eyes are, and then you'd understand, how he felt about you.

JUNE: No. He never said that to me.

ORHAN: Yes, that's what he said, "Caven te cixas xwesin." That's what those words mean.

JUNE: He was talking about Dersim.

ORHAN: He was talking about you.

JUNE: I don't believe you.

ORHAN: Do you love him?

JUNE: No. He was my friend. My church sent me.

TRACEE: Bu yer haritada yok. Onu istediğimiz yere götürebiliriz.
(*If it's not on the map, we can take her anywhere.*)

ORHAN: (*To TRACEE, in Turkish.*) Nereye gitmek istiyorsun?
(*Where do you want to go?*)

TRACEE: Diyarbakır'a. Sen yeni halı alırsın ben de Murat'ı bulurum. Kızın çok parası var ve bize muhtaç.
(*Diyarbakir. You can get carpets. I can find Murat. She's got a lot of money. She needs us.*)

ORHAN: Ne kadar parası var? Nereden biliyorsun sen parası olduğunu?
(*How much does she have? How do you know that?*)

TRACEE: Gördüm. (*I saw it.*)

JUNE: Excuse me, I don't speak Turkish so I'd appreciate it if ya'll would speak English so I can understand.

ORHAN: Do you want me to take you to Dersim?

JUNE: Yes.

ORHAN: Okay then. I'll take you. It's going to be expensive. And maybe you won't find him. Whether you find him or not I get paid.

JUNE: Just get me there.

ORHAN: (*To JUNE.*) How do you know this woman?

TRACEE: From America.

JUNE: We just met.

ORHAN: If you come with me, we're not taking her. I'm sorry, but she only makes trouble.

JUNE: Alright.

TRACEE: June, you can't go alone with this guy.

ORHAN: She cannot be trusted. She has a big mouth, and she steals. Be careful.

TRACEE: You don't believe him. June you can't believe this guy.

JUNE: How soon can we leave?

ORHAN: First thing in the morning.

The LITTLE GIRL with the scale appears. She stares at them fiercely. Lights fade out.

In dark we hear the WOLF's voice. Then we see his huge dark shadow which sometimes becomes like a man with a WOLF's head.

WOLF: Why do you want to hurt me?

You hurt me. You do me an injury.

Your mother fucked a donkey.

And so you are angry.

But don't take your anger out on our state.

You hide your tail.

But we know where it is.

It makes an ugly shape in your pants.

Look what you did!

Now these villages have to be cleaned.

See what you've done?

Forty thousand dead.

Forty thousand dead because of you.

Are you sorry? Will you say sorry?

You are in the Wolf's mouth. What do you say.

Will you speak your filthy language from inside my mouth?

Speak your filthy mule language from inside my mouth?

You've gone quiet. You've gone quiet now.

Still breathing? Are you still breathing?

We are going to separate you from your soul now.

We're going to put you under the water.

The KARAGÖZ puppet appears, very tiny, gasps for breath, floats up on the screen as if struck by a wall of water. Drowning. The LITTLE GIRL with the balance scale appears as a PUPPET.

Here's your little nurse, come to weigh what's left. Here's your little nurse.

The LITTLE GIRL PUPPET takes something from the balance scale throws it up into the sky. Fireflies sparkle briefly.

LITTLE GIRL PUPPET: Remember the fireflies. In the village.
Insects
have
electricity.
You don't.

Blackout.

Lights up. The rooftop balcony of a hotel overlooking the Sea of Marmara. A full moon. TRACEE and JUNE.

TRACEE: But he's going to kill you for all that cash. You can't go flashing your money like that. You tempt people. And you call yourself a Christian. The only thing that kept him from killing us both and taking your money, is the thought of Murat, what Murat would do. Murat inspires the fear of God in these people.

JUNE: I'm doing what God wants me to do. What happens to me doesn't matter. It's not like in Nashville. God sent me here to save Cem. I trust in God. I can hear what he's saying.

TRACEE: Where is the voice?
    You actually hear a voice inside.

JUNE: Yes.

TRACEE: A voice telling you things.

JUNE: Yes.

TRACEE: And you listen to it.
    And you take it seriously.

JUNE: Yes.

TRACEE: You hear it in your head? Like in your ears?

JUNE: In my heart.

TRACEE: You don't have ears in your heart.
    Unless you're a praying mantis.

JUNE: The praying mantis has its ear on its legs.
    To hear the frequency of bats.
    This is in my heart.
    and it's listening for God.

TRACEE: And what is the quality of this voice? Is it male? Is it female?

JUNE: I'm gonna answer you sincerely so you don't have to
mock.

TRACEE: I'm not mocking.

JUNE: Okay then. It's not quite a voice.
It's a voiceless voice.
It's like a vibration.
and I SEE the words,
and I taste them on my tongue,
in my mouth.
I find myself speaking them.
Out loud.
Then I know that it's God talking
God and not the devil.

TRACEE: There was a saint here, 560 AD
who would blow on the lettuce
from the market before he ate it,
to dislodge demons.
Byzantium was full of demons.
You can still feel them.

JUNE: Do you feel God?

TRACEE: No.

JUNE: You can feel demons but you can't feel God.
That's sad.
What a terrible state of existence.
I wish that you would be free of demons.

TRACEE: Some demons I don't want to be free of.

JUNE: I don't believe in converting people. I say, by the fruit
of the tree you will know me. If I do good works, then
people will see that Christians are good. It's the same for
being American.

TRACEE: Americans haven't done good here June.
American money funds the Turkish military.

31

Life can be really unbearable here June. Unbearable.

JUNE: Why don't you go back to America?

TRACEE: I was back.

When I was in the hospital
My leg was destroyed
I'm not the same now.
I'm not the same person I was.
I had an accident.
When I was with Murat...
I fell down.
But after that I realized
Murat really loved me
That's when I knew.
I went back to America
Without him
And I couldn't live.
He was so good,
He stayed with me in Kars,
But a hospital in Kars
Is not where you want to have steel pins
Put through your bones.
And there was an infection
From what they did to me in Kars
I came close to being crippled.
I almost died.
That was when my money ran out
And I had to go back to the states.

A WAITER has come over and hovers around them, obsessively straightening the cutlery and plates. He straightens the empty chairs. JUNE looks at him alarmed. He starts to take away a glass JUNE hasn't finished drinking.

HAYIR.

WAITER: Pardon.

He puts her plate down and exits.

TRACEE: I don't believe in God
But when I'm in trouble, I do, I pray.
I don't believe in what I'm doing
But I do it. And I pray for Murat
And even the mafia came to my door.
I said I hadn't seen him
Although we did have
one night together
before he left
And he told me he loved me
And he begged me for help
And I gave him my last
thousand dollars
because
Not only the mafia
But his whole family
Wants his skin.

The WAITER returns with a plate of watermelon.

WAITER: Karpuz. On the house.

JUNE: How do I say thank you?

WAITER: Teşekkürler.

JUNE: Teşeker...

The WAITER has walked away.

TRACEE: Say "to shake a leg" fast. It sounds just the same.
Toshakealeg.

JUNE: To shake a leg.

TRACEE: Little faster.

JUNE: Tashakealeg.

TRACEE: There's this word, bakarmısınız. You use it to get
the waiter's attention but it sounds a lot like mccarthyism.

So if you need the waiter you just say MCCARTHYISM. And he'll come.

JUNE: McCarthyism?

TRACEE: If you speak fast and confidently: MCCARTHYISM... He'll think you said bakarmısınız. Try it.

JUNE: MCCARTHYISM.

The WAITER walks over.

Toshakealeg.

WAITER: Bir şey değil. Cök Güzel. She speaks Turkish like Atatürk's daughter.

The WAITER straightens a few more things on the table.

TRACEE: He never had a daughter.

WAITER: Exactly.

JUNE: Who was Atatürk?

WAITER: Father of the Turkish Republic. God is great.

The WAITER exits.

TRACEE: You don't mess around with the Atatürk here. He made the Turkish Republic...got rid of the caliphate, the fez and the veil.

JUNE: So he freed them. Just like our President.

TRACEE: What?

JUNE: Like what we did in Afghanistan.

TRACEE raises her hand to get the WAITER's attention.

TRACEE: MCCARTHYISM.

The WAITER appears.

Istiyorum bir Rakı lütfen.

The WAITER exits.

No. It wasn't like what we did in Afghanistan. Even if he was a dictator and a killer. It was his own country to kill in.

WAITER returns with a glass of raki. She takes a big drink.

JUNE: That's not why I'm here...
I'm here because of faith and you tell me there's something missing in your life and I'm saying you can have it too, not the voices of demons, but of God, in your heart. The first place Jesus went was to the harlots. Women like you have never been excluded. Just ask. You're suffering. You are suffering now.

TRACEE: You're making me suffer.
And don't think Jesus doesn't know what you're doing. This has nothing to do with religion. You're chasing a man.

JUNE: I'm nothing like—

TRACEE: And you've put us in danger.
You went through Sultahnamet flashing your money.
There are eyes everywhere.
We could have been followed.

JUNE: A man's watching us now. Don't turn around.

TRACEE: (*Quiet and intense, to herself.*) Don't look. Don't look obvious. What if Orhan sent someone here to kill us. Or what if it's Murat. That would be a miracle. If it were Murat, I'd believe in your God. It would be a relief, I'd fall down, I would fall down at his feet, what if I could just turn right around. Oh my God oh my God let it please be Murat, let it please be Murat...

JUNE: Shut up. It's not Murat.

TRACEE: You don't know what Murat looks like.

JUNE: Is Murat black?

TRACEE turns to look at the man (GABE), who is seen for the first time in the light. He is African American. The man approaches: he looks at them in greeting and then sits at a table opposite. Stares out at the sea. The WAITER comes over.

WAITER: Are you having dinner tonight?

GABE: No. Just drinking.

WAITER: Oh. Very good. What would you like to drink?

GABE turns suddenly, sees JUNE and TRACEE who are looking at him tensely out of the corner of their eyes.

GABE: Jim Beam and Coke. How 'bout you two ladies? Can I get you something?

JUNE freezes.

Something to drink?

JUNE: No thanks.

GABE: You don't drink? Sorry. How 'bout a soda...

The WAITER exits. GABE looks at JUNE. She gets up.

TRACEE: Where are you going?

JUNE: I think I'll just visit the ladies' room.

GABE: You see the shipwreck?

JUNE: Are you talking to me?

GABE: See that dark shape? Out on the water?
A freighter's run aground. Do you see that?

JUNE: Uh huh.

GABE: (*To TRACEE.*) Have you seen the shipwreck?

TRACEE: June?

GABE: Amazing, this country. A ship goes aground and it's left to decay. Like a corpse. Ghostly.

TRACEE: It's been here forever.

GABE: It just goes to show...

JUNE starts to leave.

(*To JUNE.*) Hey, have a seat. Don't go. Did I scare you off? Sorry. I'm not, not here on the hustle.

TRACEE: Of course not.

GABE: I don't bite. I'm just being friendly.

JUNE: What brings you to Istanbul?

GABE: All the pretty tourists like you two ladies...

JUNE: So, you're here on vacation?

GABE: Business. How about you? What do you do?

JUNE: What do you think?

GABE: School teachers. Churchgoing. Here to see the Bible lands.

TRACEE: And you're here on a little R&R from Iraq.

GABE: You think I look like a soldier of fortune?

TRACEE: Nothing wrong with a man who's got a big gun...

JUNE: Do you have guns?

GABE: No, of course not.

JUNE: What do you do?

GABE: You could say I'm in the security business, I know how to keep the ladies safe.

JUNE: You're working here in Turkey?

GABE: I'm here representing some people back home. You alright?

JUNE: I'm fine.

GABE: Hey, I didn't scare you did I? I'm sorry, I don't mean to intrude. It's just so nice to talk to an American. You're from the south, like me, what's that accent. Nashville?

JUNE: And you, where are you from?

GABE: Texas, but I know some people in Nashville. Maybe we've got some friends in common.

JUNE: I doubt it.

GABE: (*Smiles.*) You think I don't go to church? You think I'm not a good God-fearing man?

JUNE: I'm sure you know your Bible.

GABE: Are you doing the whole seven churches of Anatolia thing? Have you seen the Aya Sofia? The Hagia Sophia? Church of the Divine Wisdom?

JUNE: The one built in 460 AD by Justinian?

TRACEE: She's not interested in that.

JUNE: We're leaving.

GABE: Oh, that's a shame. Where you going?

JUNE looks frozen.

TRACEE: June? Where are we going?

JUNE: I can't remember how to pronounce it.

TRACEE: Bodrum. We're going to Bodrum.

GABE: I thought you were churchgoing girls. Bodrum's the place where the sinners go.

TRACEE: Then that's where they need us.

GABE: No churches in Bodrum. You know someone there? You have a friend there?

Pause.

You're not meeting your church group there.

TRACEE: No church group.

GABE: You're meeting someone? American.

TRACEE: No, not American. I didn't come to meet Americans.

GABE: So you like a little local flavour?

TRACEE: Yes.

GABE: And what about you? What's your taste in men?

JUNE: It depends on the man. I like a man who's honest about who he is.

GABE: I like honesty too. Have you got something you want to tell me June?

JUNE: How did you know my name? We haven't been introduced.

TRACEE: I'm Tracee. This is June. Now she wants to go to Bodrum.

GABE: I'm Gabe, June. Are you sure you want to go to Bodrum? Have you considered all of the options? Because life's about choices, there might be a better choice than Bodrum.

JUNE: I know that.

TRACEE: God is telling her where to go.

GABE: Ever heard of a Cobra?

JUNE: Cobra?

GABE: You know the serpent in the garden of eden?

JUNE: The serpent?

GABE: My serpent is a Cobra. Cobra attack helicopter. But it won't attack you, I'll fly you wherever you want to go, it's faster than the bus. I have big privileges here that I'd like to share with you ladies.

JUNE: How is it you've come to have a helicopter?

TRACEE: We'd love to go with you.

JUNE: Who are you? What are you doing here?

GABE: I'm working for an aircraft company, and we just made a very big sale. And I was just looking for someone to celebrate with.

JUNE: Why aren't you celebrating with your work buddies then?

GABE: Because frankly, I needed some feminine company. I'm tired of drinking with the boys.

JUNE: Then I guess we have what you need.

GABE: Oh I think you do.

TRACEE: And what exactly would that be?

GABE: Like I said, just some feminine, attention.

TRACEE: You two, do you know each other?

JUNE: No. But he'd like to get to know us.

GABE: Yes I would.

TRACEE: Both of us.

GABE: Yeah.

TRACEE: At the same time.

JUNE: Are you the kind of man who likes a good bottle of wine?

GABE: Oh yeah.

JUNE: I mean something really good. Something—maybe something French. Something that makes a kind of, mood, that's relaxed.

GABE: Oh yeah.

JUNE: Maybe something they don't have on this menu. Something a little more special. (*To TRACEE.*) You know where he could get us something like that? I usually don't drink but it's a special occasion isn't it.

GABE: Oh yes it is. I know where I can get us something.

JUNE: So why don't you just go and do that right now. And then we can have a nice dinner together and see if we can make you feel you've had a celebration.

GABE: I'm up for that... Look, there's a place on the corner... I'll be back in a flash.

JUNE: Don't keep the ladies waiting.

GABE exits.

TRACEE: You're shaking.

JUNE: Let's go. Before he comes back.

TRACEE: June?

JUNE: Let's go to Dersim. Now. Tonight. Is there a bus?

TRACEE: You think that guy's after you?

JUNE: The money in my bag
    Is ten thousand dollars.
    I stole it from my church.
    That's all I can say. Please.
    Can I trust you?

TRACEE: Yes.

Lights out.

Shadow Puppets:

We see the inside of the WOLF's stomach as HACIVAT falls in with a scream.

HACIVAT: Agggghhh!...

He settles takes in his surroundings.

The upper GI tract of *Canis Lupus.* How unpleasant!

KARAGÖZ falls in.

KARAGÖZ: Aggggh!

He falls, settles. Sees HACIVAT.

Hacivat.

HACIVAT: Karagöz.

KARAGÖZ jumps on HACIVAT, kissing him.

No...no no no no bad touch! Bad touch!

HACIVAT shoves him off.

KARAGÖZ: Are we in heaven?

HACIVAT: No, KARAGÖZ. We're not in heaven. We're in the belly of a Wolf. Who swallowed us, because of YOU.

KARAGÖZ: Why me?

HACIVAT hits him in the head.

HACIVAT: Think.

KARAGÖZ: Oh, Oh Oh yes yes. I remember...right. Because I'm a Kurd.

HACIVAT looks around, paranoid, then in a falsely theatrical voice says:

HACIVAT: No you're not a Kurd. There's no such thing as a Kurd. You're a Turk.

KARAGÖZ: Of course I'm a Kurd, and so are you.

HACIVAT hits him. They trade blows, Punch and Judy-style.

HACIVAT: We are Turks.

KARAGÖZ: We are Kurds.

HACIVAT: We are Turks.

KARAGÖZ: Kurds.

HACIVAT: Turks.

KARAGÖZ: Kurds.

HACIVAT: Turks.

KARAGÖZ: You're a turd.

HACIVAT: That's right, we're Turds!

HACIVAT realizes KARAGÖZ has tricked him into saying something stupid. Furious he hits KARAGÖZ. This jogs his memory.

KARAGÖZ: Oh! Oh! Oh! I remember! The Wolf said I was guilty of separatist crimes. He said he would separate my body from my soul.

HACIVAT: Did he do it?

KARAGÖZ: I don't know. I don't feel my soul.

HACIVAT: Soul!

KARAGÖZ: SOUL!

Both of them frantically look through the stomach for their souls.

HACIVAT: Can you live without a soul?

KARAGÖZ: No. We have to get our souls back.

HACIVAT: I've heard they trade souls to America, for helicopters and guns.

KARAGÖZ: Let's go to America!

HACIVAT: Let's go.

KARAGÖZ: Let's go.

HAVICAT notices they are still inside the WOLF's stomach.

HACIVAT: There's a bit of a problem.

KARAGÖZ: No problem. I've got an idea.

KARAGÖZ fans a small fire.

HACIVAT: Impossible. Your head is too small for ideas.

KARAGÖZ: I'm going to set your hair on fire. And as you start to go up in flames, the Wolf will cough us out of his gullet.

HACIVAT: Excellent plan my Cro-magnon friend, but your hair is more plentiful, thus making for a greater conflagration.

KARAGÖZ: I'm not setting myself on fire.

HACIVAT: You don't have to. I'll do it for you.

KARAGÖZ: No, I'll do it for you.

HACIVAT: Please don't go to all that trouble.

KARAGÖZ: No problem brother.

KARAGÖZ pushes HACIVAT's head down on the flame explosion, they fly off the screen. On the larger screen behind we see KARAGÖZ and HACIVAT being farted out of the WOLF's behind, and flying over the skyline of Istanbul, the ocean, a large fish leaps from the ocean almost eating them. The fish falls back, then the skyline of New York appears larger and larger. KARAGÖZ and HACIVAT fall screaming into the city of New York. (Vocal improvisation helps here...)

And that's how I came to America.

Lights out.

On a bus. JUNE and TRACEE sit next to each other. They are illuminated by passing shadows. Across the aisle from them there is a WOMAN who covers her face with her hands crying quietly.

JUNE: Why did they take him?

TRACEE: No ID, they take you off the bus.

JUNE: What are they doing to him?

TRACEE: Sit down or they'll take you off the bus too.

JUNE: But what are they doing to him?

TRACEE: I don't know, I can't see.

JUNE: Where are we?

TRACEE: Outside of Urfa.

JUNE: Urfa, what's that?

TRACEE: It's the place where Abraham was born. Can you please be quiet.

JUNE: Look! Look what they're doing to him. They're beating him to death. They're killing him.

TRACEE: There's nothing you can do. Close your eyes. Close your eyes. Close your eyes and your ears.

JUNE: We've got to do something.

She gets up.

TRACEE: Nothing we can do. The police take someone, there's nothing we can do.

JUNE: Can you see him? Is he still there?

TRACEE: No, they've dragged him behind that car.

JUNE: I'm not going to let them do that to him!

JUNE moves towards door of the bus.

TRACEE: If you step off this bus, they're going to arrest you.

JUNE: (*To herself / God.*) This is what you want? This is what you want? I want to know. I want to be sure.

Waits.

I just want to understand. I'm not questioning you. I want to obey. Because I know you'd never...
What's happening out there?
Why do you. Why do you need me?
You're powerful. He's there. Blood. Why don't you do anything?
Why do you need me? I'm not questioning. You brought me for one thing, now this is something else. But I'll go. I'll do it. I just want to know. You don't say anything. But this is the time. I need your voice. I need your voice. Where is it? I want to be sure. Why don't you talk!

TRACEE: June, sit down now.

JUNE: Why don't you talk? Say something. Did I do something wrong? I've been following...did I...what did I do? I'm wrong. I was wrong.

TRACEE: June!

Long pause. JUNE comes and sits back down. A WOMAN on the bus is quietly crying.

JUNE: They should have taken me. They should have taken me instead.

TRACEE: Shhh. People are looking at you.

JUNE: (*To the WOMAN who cries.*) Did you know him?

TRACEE: June.

JUNE: Just ask her, if she knew him, what happened. In Turkish. I can't.

TRACEE: What happened, what happened back there is behind us.
It's back there now, it's gone. Okay? Gone.
There's nothing to be done.

These people survive.
They just do.
They know how.
They're strong.
They're stronger than us.
They're used to it.

WOMAN: I speak English.

TRACEE: Oh.

WOMAN: I am a teacher of English. I can hear you.

TRACEE: I'm sorry. I'm sorry.

WOMAN: You say I'm used to this?

JUNE: Were you with him?

TRACEE: Just leave her alone.

JUNE: We're American, we want to help. Can you understand?

WOMAN: Your English I understand, your stupidity I don't.

JUNE: Can I sit by you?

JUNE moves across the aisle to the WOMAN.

I lost somebody too. I lost someone too. He was taken. Taken. That's why I'm here. To find him.

TRACEE: June. June. Get back over here.

JUNE: I know how you feel. I feel the same way.

WOMAN: Do you?

JUNE: Can I help, can I do anything? I made a mistake. I should have told them they can't...can't do that...to a human being.

WOMAN: Why didn't you?

Pause.

I should go back to help him, but I'm going to see my husband in Muş. And I have something with me I can't...

JUNE: Is he working there?

Pause.

Is he working? Your husband? He has a job in this place Muş?

WOMAN: No. He's in jail.

JUNE: Why?

WOMAN: His political activities. He's been in jail for five years.

JUNE: I'm sorry. Is he innocent?

WOMAN: Innocent. Would you like to see his picture?

She passes a photo to JUNE and then TRACEE.

JUNE: He's a prisoner, this picture was taken in prison.

The WOMAN takes out another picture.

WOMAN: This picture was taken last month.

JUNE: But, this isn't...this is from before.

WOMAN: Look at his face. Look he has black and blue, sunken eyes.

JUNE: But, he's...he's got a uniform.

WOMAN: Of the guerrillas.

JUNE: He's on a mountain.

WOMAN: Yes.

JUNE: He's got a—

WOMAN: Kalashnikov.

JUNE: Why?

WOMAN: I did it with Photoshop. This picture. So I can see him where he should be—the mountains. Not where they are keeping him now. If he gets out, we will go to America.

TRACEE: You'll never get a visa.

WOMAN: If they know what happened, if they know. I am sure, America can help us.

JUNE: How?

WOMAN: Like what you did in Iraq.

TRACEE: Americans don't even know about you. Nobody cares. And they have their own problems.

JUNE: It's not that we don't care, we just don't know what to do. We'd do something, if we knew how to help.

WOMAN: Do you want to help me?

JUNE: But what can I do?

WOMAN: My cousin was taking this package to our village. It's three hours north of Diyarbekir. Would you take it for me? If I go back, the Jandarma will take it...

TRACEE: What's in the bag?

WOMAN: A radio...some music. Cassettes. And clothes. From friends in Istanbul. for the people, for the families who are staying in the village.

TRACEE: What village? Where?

WOMAN: Near Dersim.

JUNE: Dersim. Dersim... Dersim. That's where we're going.

WOMAN: You know it? It's beautiful there.

TRACEE: Clothes and cassettes. So why would the Jandarma take that from you?

WOMAN: That's how they are.

JUNE: There are a lot of turtlenecks.

WOMAN: Yes. It gets cold in the mountains.

JUNE: Black. No color.

WOMAN: If you wear color, then people can see you.
In the mountains, you don't want anyone to see you.
Can you understand?

JUNE: I'll take the bag.

TRACEE: What if there are messages for the rebels in there.
(*Whispers.*) The PKK.

JUNE: I'll take the bag if you can help me find who I'm
looking for.

The WOMAN writes down a number on a scrap of paper.

WOMAN: I have someone who can help you, no problem. If
you take my package, I have a cousin who will meet you
at the Diyarbekir Otogar. I can call him. He'll take you
from the bus. It's in the mountains, beautiful mountains.

JUNE: I remember, he said, I miss my mountains, I am
missing my village. He told me, he told me they have a
wedding for the sheep.

TRACEE: A wedding for the sheep.

JUNE: In the fall. When he was a kid. He was a shepherd.
When they put the sheep together. I remember he said,
the males and the females, when they put them together,
they have a big celebration, a feast, and he said, it's just
like a wedding. He had pictures of the rams, their horns
were painted blue. We were laughing.

JUNE turns away and stares into the dark.

WOMAN: Lady. You are right, that's how it is there.

JUNE: That's where we have to go.

Lights out.

Shadow Puppets:

Street scene. New York.

KARAGÖZ falls from the sky screaming. Just before he hits the ground, he freezes.

KOOLIOZ is seen pushing a cart and selling soul food.

KOOLIOZ: Soul food! Soul food! Sweet potato pie! Fried chicken. Collard greens. Grits and gravy. Soul food! (*He goes off.*)

KARAGÖZ falls screaming from the sky. Bounces. Lands. Jumps up. Looks around.

The LITTLE GIRL PUPPET with the scale crosses the scene:

LITTLE GIRL PUPPET: Spare change. Spare change?

KARAGÖZ: Is this America? Is this America?

LITTLE GIRL PUPPET: Any help? Any food? Spare change?

She exits.

KARAGÖZ: (*He cries in despair.*) Where is Hacivat? Where is my soul?

KOOLIOZ enters.

KOOLIOZ: Soul food! Soul food! Sweet potato pie. Chitlins. Soul food.

KARAGÖZ: Hey hey hey... Is that food for the soul?

KOOLIOZ: (*A plate of soul food floats before KARAGÖZ appears.*) Yes it is my brother. Only five dollars.

KARAGÖZ tries to take the plate. It floats away each time he reaches for it.

Five dollars a plate.

KARAGÖZ tries to grab the food. KOOLIOZ hits KARAGÖZ. The plate of food floats up in the air, flips several times and lands on KOOLIOZ's head.

You act like one o'them lost souls man, get outta here.

Kicks him. KARAGÖZ *backs away hides behind a lamp post, crying.*

HACIVAT *falls from the sky screaming. Lands.*

What the hell?

He goes back to hawking soul food.

Soul food, soul food, Fried chicken. Get your hot soul food here.

KARAGÖZ *hides but watches* HACIVAT.

HACIVAT: Is this food for the soul?

KOOLIOZ: Yes it is my brother. Five dollars.

HACIVAT: It'll make the soul good? It'll bring the soul close?

KOOLIOZ: Affirmative.

HACIVAT: Here's five dollars my good man.

KOOLIOZ: Thank you. Here you go.

He gives him the plate of food.

KOOLIOZ *exits.*

KARAGÖZ: (*From behind the lamp post.*) Hacivat, and food!

HACIVAT: You know, I thought I heard something.

KARAGÖZ: (*In a high fake voice.*) HACIVAT. I am your soul.

HACIVAT: My soul! My soul! I've been looking all over for you.

KARAGÖZ: Have you got any food for me?

HACIVAT: Yes, my soul I do!

KARAGÖZ: Go around the corner and leave it.

HACIVAT: How do I know that you're really my soul?

KARAGÖZ: Because souls know everything about you. You had a friend. His name was Karagöz.

HACIVAT: Yes! Yes!

KARAGÖZ: He was very intelligent. Well hung. A terrific dancer.

HACIVAT: Yes! But where is he? Where is he?

KARAGÖZ: Eat first. Talk later.

HACIVAT puts the plate of food on the ground.

HACIVAT: Yes. Yes. I am setting the plate of food on the ground now and I am backing away in a backwards fashion.

HACIVAT backs away. KARAGÖZ floats above him and then descends on the food.

KARAGÖZ: Yes!

He devours the plate face down like an animal. Burps.

HACIVAT sees KARAGÖZ on the ground.

HACIVAT: KARAGÖZ!

KARAGÖZ: Hacivat!

They kiss.

HACIVAT: Have you seen my soul? I left a plate of food for him, now he's gone.

KARAGÖZ: (*Still in soul's high voice.*) No, I didn't see your soul.

HACIVAT: (*Realizes what KARAGÖZ has done.*) You idiot! Now my soul will go hungry.

KOOLIOZ: Soul food, soul food, get your hot chitlins here!

HACIVAT: Listen, my good man, we've lost our souls and we need a little more soul food to lure them hither.

KOOLIOZ holds his hand out out for money.

But we haven't had time to exchange our currency.

KOOLIOZ: You boys illegal?

HACIVAT: We're both in excellent health.

KOOLIOZ: Gotta green card? You need a job under the table?

KARAGÖZ: What's a job?

HACIVAT: Under what table? We are very tall men!

KOOLIOZ takes HACIVAT close and whispers in his ear.

Why are we whispering?

KOOLIOZ: Homeland Security man. They got ears everywhere. Listen.

He whispers again.

KARAGÖZ: What's a job? What's a job? What's a job!

HACIVAT: It's a place where you meet many beautiful girls.

KARAGÖZ: What about food?

KOOLIOZ: All the food you can eat.

KARAGÖZ: Let's go there!

KOOLIOZ whistles.

KOOLIOZ: See that truck over there? Just climb in the back. You'll be headed to Florida, very good jobs...

KARAGÖZ: If this job's so great, why don't you do it?

KOOLIOZ: I already got two jobs.

HACIVAT: In America, jobs are so great everyone has two!

KARAGÖZ: But what about our souls?

KOOLIOZ: Get a job you can buy yourself soul food.

KARAGÖZ: Let's go. Get a job!

HACIVAT: And be rich!

KARAGÖZ, KOOLIOZ, HACIVAT exit. The LITTLE GIRL PUPPET reappears. a truck whizzes by. We see that KARAGÖZ and HACIVAT are inside the wheels—their bodies contorted into rings as the truck rolls by.

LITTLE GIRL PUPPET: Spare change? Any help. Spare change?

End of scene.

Diyarbekir bus station. JUNE and TRACEE in the middle of a parking lot. A CHILD circles them.

TRACEE: There's nobody here, he didn't show up.

JUNE: She gave me the number in case he was late.

TRACEE takes the number.

CHILD: Hello.

JUNE: Hello.

CHILD: Hello money.

TRACEE: Murat can help you. Murat has connections—he's here. Orhan said he was here, I'm sure we can find him.

CHILD: Hello money.

JUNE: That's good, you'll get to see him again. I have to go with this man.

CHILD: Hello money.

TRACEE: How are you going to communicate? I speak the language, you don't.

CHILD: Hello money. America?

JUNE: No.

CHILD: Hello money America.

JUNE: No America.

CHILD: What is your name? Money? Money?

BAWER appears, he speaks to the CHILD.

BAWER: Bese. (***Enough.***)

CHILD: Hello money.

BAWER: Bese! Bese!

CHILD: Money!

BAWER gives the CHILD money. The CHILD doesn't leave.

BAWER: Hello, I am Bawer.

JUNE: I'm June.

BAWER: My cousin said you would have a present for me. Is that it?

JUNE: Your cousin said you can help me find my friend. He's in Dersim. His name is Cem Yildiz.

BAWER: Is he in Tunceli?

JUNE: Dersim.

BAWER: Tunceli is Dersim. The Turks renamed it.

JUNE: In Dersim. By the Munzur river.

BAWER: Which one? There are two. Where on the river?

JUNE: I don't know.

BAWER: What village?

JUNE: I thought it was... Caven te cixas...

BAWER: What?

JUNE: I was wrong.

BAWER: How are you going to find this person?

JUNE: I don't know, just take me to Dersim.

BAWER: But where in Dersim? Lady. The city? The city of Tunceli? Is that what you want? The minute you get there, they'll write down your name and follow you wherever you go. There's more army and police there than the whole civilian population.

JUNE: Not the city, the mountains.

BAWER: Which mountains? Baba Manzur? Duzgun Baba? Where?

JUNE: His aşiret is Kureyşan.

BAWER: That's many people in Dersim. How can I help you?

She takes out a diary, handwritten.

JUNE: The last time I saw him he gave this to me. It's something he wrote. He asked me to keep it for him. I haven't shown it to anyone else...he wrote it. I think it might be something very personal.

BAWER: This is Kurmanci.

JUNE: He just said, could I keep this for him. I wasn't sure if I should look at it or not. I wasn't sure if it was for me. I think he wanted me to have it for some reason, I don't know, maybe it says where he is. I think it would be alright with him if I showed it to you. If I let you read it.

TRACEE: Why the hell didn't you use this before?

JUNE: You wouldn't understand.

BAWER looks at it hard. He turns the pages.

BAWER: He wrote many things.

Pause.

JUNE: Is there anything,
   Is there anything?
   What is it?
   Is there something in there that can help us to find him?
   Something that can help?

BAWER: I can't read it.

JUNE: You can tell me anything. I just want to know.

BAWER: No I can't read my own language. We don't learn this in school. I'm illiterate in my own language. But I'm going to learn.

TRACEE: Murat would know how to read it.

CHILD: Hello money.

BAWER: Bese! CI BU!

CHILD: Money!

BAWER: There are people who can read this. I can take you to them. In the mountains. If you're coming, let's go.

He reaches for the bag.

TRACEE is looking through the book.

JUNE: I need to ask you first, about this package. Will someone get hurt because of this?

Pause.

Is there something in here that can someone get killed?

BAWER: We're in a war.

JUNE: I thought it was just, some clothes, and cassettes and this tape player. Is there something else?

BAWER: Don't ask.

JUNE: Something that can kill someone? If I'm going with you, I need to know.

CHILD: Hello money.

BAWER: Then don't come. It's okay. Thank you for bringing my present.

JUNE: If there's something in here that can kill someone then I'm sorry, I can't give it to you.

CHILD: Hello money.

TRACEE sees someone, off. She walks off. JUNE doesn't notice, distracted by the CHILD.

BAWER: You see this kid? Why is she begging?

JUNE: I don't know, but killing just makes everything worse.

BAWER: I know her family. They came from Lice. The army shot her father. He was a shepherd. But he wouldn't be a village guard. Her village was burned. So they lost their animals, their land and their house. Her mother was forced to came to Diyarbekir with nothing. They live in one cinderblock room, seven kids. No running water.

No electricity. They beg. These people were proud, they didn't need anyone. What happened to them? Everything, even their language has been taken from them. There are three million people like her in this country. And people look down on them, scream at them: shame. But all of us are living like this, in exile. What should we do?

JUNE: I can't give you something that gets people killed.

BAWER: What would you do if you were in our position?

CHILD: Hello money.

BAWER: What would you do?

CHILD: Hello money. America.

JUNE: Get away! Get out of here! Scram!

BAWER: If you don't have an answer then give me my package.

CHILD: Hello money. Money? Money?

BAWER: Should we beg? Should we pray? While our history's erased? Should we say that we never existed at all.

CHILD: Hello Money. America. Money.

JUNE: This tape recorder is full of plastic explosives.

CHILD: Hello money.

JUNE: Get away stupid brat. I'll hit you. Go home.

BAWER: If you don't have an answer then give that to me.

She hands him the bag.

JUNE: I want to go with you.

BAWER: Alright then. Let's go. You can't live your life in the rearview mirror. When is it going to hit you again. You have to go on, to keep driving forward.

JUNE: What hit you? Something hit you?

BAWER: Last September nationalists bombed near here. Ten people were killed. Mostly kids. I saw it. There was blood up to the sixth story of a building. But you can't think about what's coming up behind you, you can't take a breath, you just have to go on.

JUNE: What is coming up behind you?

BAWER: It can cause some slight kind of depression, no, some serious serious heavy psychological depression. Let's go.

TRACEE and MURAT enter, behind BAWER.

MURAT: Sweet, who is your friend?

Pause, TRACEE looks at him mistrustfully.

I was working in Iraq, that's why I never got your messages till now. Sweet, I've work for Americans. We have our own Kurdistan there. America gave it to us.

JUNE: Tracee?

MURAT: Sweet. Introduce me to your friend.

Lights out. End of Act One.

Act Two

TRACEE, JUNE, BAWER, in Bawer's car. They are driving.

TRACEE: Oh my God, oh my God.

JUNE: Is that a tank?

BAWER: Ignore it. Don't make eye contact with the soldiers.

TRACEE: We didn't even get to have sex.

JUNE: Why? Why did he run away like that?

TRACEE: TAKE US TO HASANKEYF.

BAWER: Look, Lady, I'm not your chauffeur.

TRACEE: No. You have to take me to Hasankeyf. Murat took Cem's notebook. I'm sorry. He took it. I gave it to him. He understands it. He'll read it. I told you he could, I told you he could.

JUNE quickly rummages through her bag, franticaly, realizes she doesn't have the notebook.

JUNE: What the hell did you do!

TRACEE: I'm protecting you.

JUNE: Can we go to Hasankeyf please?

TRACEE: You can't go running around like this...

BAWER: We're going to Dersim.

TRACEE: (*Imitating JUNE.*) Please interpret my notebook in Kurdish, you don't know this guy, you don't know who he is.

BAWER: Then get out of the car!

TRACEE: Murat can read it, Murat is going to help. And I guess he needs your money.

JUNE: What?

TRACEE: The money you stole from your church, he needs it. It's so anti American here and Murat has been working for the Americans. There are people who want him dead. So he went to Hasankeyf.

BAWER: You get out of the car. (*To JUNE.*) I'll take you to Dersim. I don't have time. Hasankeyf is two hours away, the OPPOSITE direction of where we're going.

TRACEE: We have to go there. That's where he's gone.

JUNE: I have to get that book. It's all I've got left of him. Please. I have to go get that book.

BAWER: No. Enough. Get out of the car. Both of you.

JUNE: What are all those big black planes in the sky?

BAWER: American planes use our air bases here, they're flying to Iraq. Maybe they can help you. What is it with you Americans? You think your problems are more important than everything. You bring them to my country. Your boyfriends, your bombs. I have something I need to take to the mountains. They need it. Bese enough!

JUNE: I can't let something happen to Cem's notebook. I promised.

BAWER: I'm stopping the car. I want you both out.

JUNE: No. Wait. Please.

BAWER: I'll take you to Dersim but she has to go.

TRACEE: You can't leave me.

BAWER: Crazy women. I can't take you both.

JUNE: Listen, what if this book, what if it's something that has to be saved?

TRACEE: Murat wrote his life story in Kurdish but his mother found it and burned it in the stove.

JUNE: But how many books have been written in Kurdish, it's important.

BAWER: We don't need that now, that's useless, what we need is to get this package to the mountains. NOW. Get out of my car please.

JUNE: It's the only chance I have of ever finding him.

BAWER: Why don't you check with the police or the hospitals?

TRACEE: If we don't get there tonight, I don't know what Murat's going to do.

JUNE: He called me, he said he was in hiding, he said he was afraid he was going to be deported.

BAWER: Lady—I'm sorry.

JUNE: I said Cem that's impossible. You've got a green card, you already had political asylum, and he said, no retroactively, they revoked it, they say I'm a terrorist.

BAWER: We have so many stories like this...

JUNE: I told him it couldn't be real. It was just a mistake.

BAWER: That's where you catch the bus back to town.

JUNE: I went to see him, at this motel, I said Cem, what are you doing here? And he gave me his book. He was afraid. He said he wanted to stay with me, a couple of days, he needed to hide. I said, that's crazy. Just go to the government people, talk to them. Straighten it out. You didn't do anything wrong. They already gave you political asylum. And he said, everything I did to get political asylum is what is getting me deported right now. He said, could he hide at my apartment. Just a few days. And I said no.

BAWER: I'm sorry, but people are counting on me.

JUNE: I let it happen. I really need to find him. This notebook, might be the last chance I have.

BAWER: Get out of the car.

JUNE: I'll give you ten thousand dollars.

BAWER: What?

JUNE: If you can get Cem's notebook back, I can give you
ten thousand dollars. I have it right here in my bag.

TRACEE: You can't do that.

JUNE: I have to get that notebook.

BAWER: Okay lady, that's fair. (*To TRACEE.*) So this Murat has
gone to Hasankeyf.

TRACEE: You can't do that. I can't believe you did that.
(*To BAWER.*) But you can't hurt Murat, please don't hurt
Murat.

BAWER: All he has to do is give her the book. Why should he
get hurt? I'll turn the car around.

TRACEE: But that money, that's to help Murat.

BAWER: Where in Hasakeyf? Where will he be?

TRACEE: That money's for Murat, to get out of the country.
We have to help him. I can't live without Murat, you have
to understand.

BAWER: Okay. We're going to Hasankeyf. Happy?

TRACEE: When I first came back from this country
I could only paint Murat.
Like he was right there under my eyelids.
He was the only thing I could see.
And when my husband saw these paintings he said
Your work has become so alive.
It is good you have a muse.
He said this so innocently.
As if he couldn't see that Murat
Had written his name on my skin
And all over my body
The words "She is mine"
"She is ruined for everything but me
She won't be with you anymore.

I am living in her head now
So tell her goodbye."
I gave up everything to be here.
There was nothing else I could do.

JUNE: I understand you.

TRACEE: How can that be?

JUNE: Because he makes you feel closer to God and we'll do anything to get that feeling.

TRACEE: This has nothing to do with God.

JUNE: Anything that makes us feel closer to God...

TRACEE: When we were in Kars, I tried to leave. I hurt Murat then.

JUNE: Cem once said, "If you go to my village, I've touched every rock. I've touched every tree. I am there, even if they don't see me."

TRACEE: I tried to leave and he threw me down the stairs. My leg was shattered, but that's when I knew he loved me. The man you're looking for can't be helped. Only Murat. Only Murat.

BAWER: (*To TRACEE.*) You are thinking too much about love. You are thinking too much of one person. One person can't matter now.
Do you know anything about where we're going?
It's a castle over the Tigris river.
People have lived there ten thousand years. Thirty three civilizations were there. There's a castle that goes straight up to the sky. It's paradise.
But next year it will all disappear.
Seventy thousand people will all lose their houses.
They are building a dam, the Ilisu dam.
It will all go underwater.

JUNE: Why?

BAWER: They can control the water to Iraq, they dam the
Tigris, they can cut off the water. Because, they don't want
a Kurdistan there. They say they don't want a Kurdistan,
not even in Argentina. You know what they say about
Kurdish villages? They say, they have to be cleaned. This
is the way they clean us. By drowning. That's how much
they are afraid. So when we come to Hasankeyf, you
will see something that is going to disappear. A German
company, Siemens is funding it.

So we'll put your ten thousand dollars to good use.

Blackout.

Shadow Puppets:

HACIVAT, KARAGÖZ, KOOLIOZ outside a church.

KARAGÖZ: What is this place?

KOOLIOZ: Nashville. Our truck broke down.

HACIVAT: My good man, who were those strange men pursuing us with black sticks and guns?

KOOLIOZ: That's the police man. You're illegal here.

KARAGÖZ: Huh?

KOOLIOZ: You're aliens man. You're against the law.

KARAGÖZ: What about you?

KOOLIOZ: I'm just black.

HACIVAT: What is this place with the very tall tower.

KOOLIOZ: It's a church. It's a house of God, man.

KARAGÖZ: God lives there?

KOOLIOZ: No. Homeless people.

HACIVAT: What's that?

KOOLIOZ: People who don't have no home. Like us. When we get inside do as I do and say as I say.

They enter: inside the church. A MINISTER appears:

MINISTER: Do you take the Lord Jesus Christ as your savior?

KOOLIOZ: Yes I do.

MINISTER: Here's your blanket and bread. (*To HACIVAT.*) Do you take the Lord Jesus Christ as your savior?

HACIVAT: Yes I do.

MINISTER: Here is your blanket and bread. (*To KARAGÖZ.*) Do you take the Lord Jesus Christ as your Savior?

KARAGÖZ: Never the met the man, but thanks for the blanket.

KOOLIOZ: He doesn't speak English.

MINISTER: Okey dokey. Sweet dreams.

They lay down and sleep. HACIVAT and KOOLIOZ snore. KARAGÖZ cries. The MOON enters. She floats over KARAGÖZ.

MOON: Karagöz, why are you crying?

KARAGÖZ: Why is the moon talking to me?

MOON: In America, anything is possible Karagöz. Do you want to come with me in a dream?

KARAGÖZ: Yes.

The MOON lifts him up and they fly away together. KARAGÖZ straddles the cresent moon as they fly across the sky.

MOON: Hang on Karagöz.

KARAGÖZ: Like this? Is this the right position?

MOON: Oh yes.

KARAGÖZ: It's good for you?!

MOON: Yesss! Do you want to see America!

KARAGÖZ: Yes!

The MOON flies wildly.

MOON / KARAGÖZ: Whooooo!

MOON: I'll show you everything!

KARAGÖZ: Moon, I'm not speaking English right now, how come you understand me.

MOON: I don't know.

KARAGÖZ: Maybe we talk with our bodies.

MOON: No Karagöz. I don't have a body.

KARAGÖZ: I think you do. I feel your body Moon. It's beautiful.

MOON: (*Shyly.*) No...

69

KARAGÖZ: How else can we talk?

MOON: Maybe in America, they understand all languages.

KARAGÖZ: Wow.

MOON: Do you want to learn English? I can be your teacher.

Below them the street scene comes into view. They see two small figures...a COP, maybe he's two-headed like a monster, and KOOLIOZ. The COP is beating KOOLIOZ.

KARAGÖZ: Hey! Hey! What's that!

The MOON stops in her tracks. she moves down closer to the COP.

MOON: You stop that right now!

TWO-HEADED COP: Lady! We had a report of possible alien activity here.

MOON: I don't believe in aliens officer.

TWO-HEADED COP: Illegal aliens. Terrorist suspects. You seen anyone? Funny accents? Dark skin?

KOOLIOZ: (*Who has been trying to sneak away.*) Dark skin? Hello?

MOON: Why are you beating him?

KOOLIOZ: I'm black.

TWO-HEADED COP: No ID.

MOON: But this is America. We don't need ID. We're free.

KOOLIOZ: I'm not. Three million of me in jail.

MOON: That's why it's America. We're a free country.

TWO-HEADED COP: Thank you for reminding me. You are so right. Hey, what's that shadow I see? You hiding someone?!

MOON: Bye!

She flies away. The TWO-HEADED COP and KOOLIOZ disappear.

KARAGÖZ: Wow. That was good. Hey! What's that! What are all those big knockers down there?

MOON: Those are the Hollywood hills.

KARAGÖZ: Wow...

MOON: There's Las Vegas!

KARAGÖZ: Look there's my donkey!...donkey! What are you doing in Las Vegas? Hey donkey, why are you working for someone else? I thought they shot him. I'm glad you're alive! But why doesn't he recognize me?

MOON: Maybe he's only a memory. Look! There's the Rocky mountains.

KARAGÖZ: Hey. They have sheep there.

MOON: Of course they have sheep.

Faint sound of Kurdish music is heard.

KARAGÖZ: Hey, hey, are we back in the village? I can see everything. Look, there's my sister! Hey! I'm coming. Make me some tea! Hey! I'm an important man in America. I'm rich. With a beautiful wife. A big house. Someday I'll send you a ticket. First class! How come she doesn't answer me.

MOON: Karagöz, that's just a memory.

KARAGÖZ: But I see her so clearly. It's like she's right there!

MOON: Only because you're so far away. That's how memory is.

KARAGÖZ: But it's real, it's not an illusion.

MOON: It's real but it's gone. It happened before. Your memories stop you from seeing America.

KARAGÖZ: I want to go home.

MOON: Then why did you come here?

KARAGÖZ: The Wolf took our souls for helicopters and guns. He sent them here. My soul is gone. I'm empty.

MOON: You're right. Karagöz, you have to go to the White House and tell them.

KARAGÖZ: What's that?

MOON: It's where the president lives. If the Wolf took your soul, you have to tell the president.

KARAGÖZ: Why?

MOON: Just tell him what happened. He'll fix it.

KARAGÖZ: Ummm. Somehow I don't think that's a good idea.

MOON: He'll understand.

KARAGÖZ: But the Wolf.

MOON: The Wolf can't hurt you here. We have laws.

KARAGÖZ: Um… Okay… Where is this White House?

MOON: It's in Washington DC. I'll show you. Let's go.

They fly off together. End of scene.

Hasankeyf. TRACEE *stands at the edge of the cliff looking down on the Tigris.*

MURAT: Sweet, don't stand so close to the edge.

TRACEE: I thought I'd never find you again.

MURAT: We will always find each other. What is that word? Psychic. Psychic energy. You have it. And it pulls us together.

TRACEE: Yes.

MURAT: You remember it right? Come away from the edge.

He edges closer to her.

If you're quiet, you can hear the river on the wind.

TRACEE: There. There's the Tigris. Mesopotamia. It's funny. When I was little. We'd hear about this place in school. Mesopotamia. The cradle of civilization. I didn't know it was real, it was just a place in my imagination.

MURAT: Sweet, did you bring something for me?

TRACEE: I always bring something for you.

MURAT: Yes. Come here.

TRACEE: We'll go away together now?

MURAT: Everything comes with money.

TRACEE: I don't have it.

MURAT: Sweet. Where is your friend?

TRACEE: She's coming. I told her to give me a minute. I had to see you alone.

MURAT: Sweet. Go and get her.

TRACEE: I couldn't find you.

MURAT: We will always find each other.

TRACEE: I was in agony.

MURAT: I was in Iraq.

TRACEE: Agony.

MURAT: I saw twenty men blown up right in front of me. First they were there, then they were gone.

TRACEE: What about you, are you going away?

MURAT: We will go together.

TRACEE: Where?

MURAT: I'm getting a visa for Europe, from the mafia. Eight thousand dollars.

TRACEE: You'll go without me.

MURAT: You can come to me after I get there.

TRACEE: I'll never hear from again. You'll disappear. Till there's something you need from me. You know I'll always get it for you if I can, anything. Everything for you.

MURAT: Sweet be careful, you are right on the edge. Go get your friend for me sweet. You shouldn't have left her alone.

TRACEE: You're right. She shouldn't be alone. I just needed to see you first before...

MURAT: Sweet, you have an American passport. You can go anywhere. Who will give me a visa? No one. I have to leave. I have to buy one on the black market. Nobody wants me.

TRACEE: I want you.

MURAT: I can only go to Iraq. No country will take me. Where can I go?

TRACEE: America. We can get married.

MURAT: I've had enough marriage. Sweet. I have to leave now or they're going to kill me.

TRACEE: Who? Your wife? Your ten other girlfriends?

MURAT: Sweet, try and make some emotional control. Go and bring me your friend.

TRACEE: I'll never see you again.

MURAT: Sweet. Help me. Please.

TRACEE: I want to be free. I want to fly.

MURAT: Come here.

TRACEE: I want to have one beautiful moment. One. One moment of flight.

MURAT: I can make you fly.

TRACEE: I remember. I know.

TRACEE steps off the edge of the cliff and disappears.

MURAT goes to the edge and looks over. He steps back in shock. Then he goes away from the edge and sits down.

JUNE enters.

JUNE: Roj Baş. (*Hello.*)

MURAT: Roj Baş. (*Hello.*)

JUNE: Çawani. (*How are you?*)

MURAT: Başim. Tu Çawayi? (*I'm good. And you?*)

JUNE: Başim. Hewa jî gelek başe.
(*Good. The weather is beautiful.*)

MURAT: Tu jî gelek bedawîyî gelek sîrînî. Tu min famdiki.
(*You are very nice, very sweet. You understand me.*)

JUNE: I'm afraid my language lesson ended there.

MURAT: You speak very sweetly.

JUNE: No.

MURAT: Like a traditional woman.

JUNE: Where is Tracee? I want to see her.

MURAT: I'm not going to hurt you.

JUNE: I know.

MURAT: How did you learn Kurdish?

JUNE: From my friend. He's waiting for us. He didn't want me to come up alone, but I said I'd be fine.

MURAT: I'd never hurt anyone. Really, I'm weak.

JUNE: That's not a weakness.

MURAT: Yes it is. We weren't wild like everyone else. You have to be willing to kill without feeling.

JUNE: Why?

MURAT: To have our own nation.

JUNE: What good is a nation if it's just like all the others?

MURAT: Well, it would be ours.

JUNE: Does it matter? Does everyone deserve that?

MURAT: You have yours, does it matter to you?

JUNE: I don't know.

MURAT: You killed the Indians. Lived off the slaves and grabbed up all the oil in the world. And I'm saying we have to be more like you. Maybe you have to kill people to help them. That's how you made your nation. People have to die for democracy.

JUNE: I don't believe that.

MURAT: Some people have to die, then the world becomes different. So it's worth it. Isn't that what you think?

JUNE: I'm Christian.

MURAT: So Jesus died right? Jesus had to die.

JUNE: Jesus wanted to die.

MURAT: How do you know, did he tell you?

JUNE: Yes.

MURAT: Then why don't you ask him what's in this book?

JUNE: Because he doesn't read Kurmanci. Do you?

MURAT: Yes.

JUNE: You read it?

MURAT: Come to Germany with me. I'll tell you everything.

JUNE: Tell me now.

MURAT: His whole life.

JUNE: Tell me what's there that will help me to find him.

MURAT: I'll tell you in Germany.

JUNE: What about Tracee?

MURAT: Please. Come to Germany with me. You are not going to find this man now.

JUNE: You didn't read it! You're lying to me.

MURAT: I can tell you everything. I can give you the truth.

JUNE: The truth about what? Why is he gone? What did he do?

MURAT: He was too funny about the wrong things. That's all.

JUNE: What do you mean?

MURAT: Come to Germany with me I'll read the whole thing. I'll tell you what he wrote. Sentence by sentence.

JUNE: Just give me the notebook now.

MURAT: I need money... I need it for a visa. I have to have it. Really, you could save my life... He wrote many things about you.

JUNE: You're lying.

MURAT: Every thought he had about you.

JUNE: Can you tell me the name of his village?

MURAT: Torunoba. It's just outside of Ovacik.

JUNE: How do I get there?

MURAT: It's off the road from Tunceli. But you'll never make it...

JUNE: Yes I will. That's why I need the money. It's for Cem. To help Cem.

MURAT: You stole from your church, now I'm stealing from you.

JUNE: Tracee told you that?

MURAT: Tracee told me how good and how generous, a helper of people. A very good person.

JUNE: Do you think he went back to the village? Don't you think he's hiding?

MURAT: There's no where to hide. In Dersim? In Ovacik? He'd never get there. They'd take him. You too, if you try to go. Do you have the money here?

JUNE: Yes.

MURAT: I need it. If you want this book. Give it to me.

He takes a step towards JUNE. BAWER appears.

BAWER: June come.

JUNE: It's okay.

BAWER: June, you have to come now.

JUNE: Why?

BAWER: (*In Turkish.*) Ona daha fazla yaklaşma.
(***Don't get any closer to her.***)

MURAT: (*In Kurdish.*) Tistek nine biraye qicik, em dizanin hun taybetin. Tera lazim nine giringa xwe, nisanbidi.

(*It's all right little brother, we know you are special. You don't have to show how important you are.*)

BAWER: Makuro—Tu duxazi ez mejiyete berdem ser çavete?
(*You want me to put your brain on top of your eyes?*)

MURAT: I'll give you the answer.

He moves closer to JUNE.

BAWER: June, let's go.

JUNE: I'm not going without my notebook.

JUNE moves towards MURAT, he gestures, it is clear they are about to have some kind of confrontation—physical, on the edge of the cliff.

JUNE, MURAT and BAWER fade; as they do, we see momentarily, only their shadows.

Shadow Puppets:

Kitchen of a Turkish restaurant. KOOLIOZ is wearing a chef's hat. KARAGÖZ sleeps with his head in a tub of butter.

KARAGÖZ: Yes moon yes!

KOOLIOZ: Ahhh hemmmm.

KARAGÖZ: Oh goooood moooon mmmmm. Fly. Fly to the White House. Let's tell the president.

> *KOOLIOZ kicks KARAGÖZ in the ass. KARAGÖZ wakes up.*

KOOLIOZ: You illegal alien, they won't let you in the White House. Been here five years you still don't speak English.

KARAGÖZ: Can you go to the White house and tell them the Wolf took my soul?

KOOLIOZ: Course I can. My ancestors built it.

KARAGÖZ: And they'll let you in…and they'll listen to you.

KOOLIOZ: They might even make me President.

KARAGÖZ: President of dishwashers.

KOOLIOZ: Leader of this country.

KARAGÖZ: Leader of the free nation of fried chicken.

KOOLIOZ: Do you want to go to the White House or not?

KARAGÖZ: How can we get there? We still don't have money.

KOOLIOZ: Steal a car.

KARAGÖZ: Let's go then.

KOOLIOZ: Shhh. Here comes the boss.

> *HACIVAT enters. KOOLIOZ exits.*

KARAGÖZ: That's not a boss, that's a worm on two legs.

HACIVAT: KARAGÖZ! You have ten thousand pounds of butter to stack.

> *Shouts after KOOLIOZ.*

SHADOW LANGUAGE: ACT TWO

And you! Wash the dishes!

KARAGÖZ: Hacivat, what about our souls?

HACIVAT: Keep working. In ten years we'll buy ourselves new ones.

Sound of a car horn honking. Then a siren.

What's that?!

A police car appears floating in the sky. KOOLIOZ is driving.

KOOLIOZ: KARAGÖZ! Let's go!

KARAGÖZ runs, jumps inside the police car.

HACIVAT: Wait! Where are you going!

He runs after them, jumps on the roof of the car.

KARAGÖZ / KOOLIOZ: Off to the White House! Off to Washington!

KOOLIOZ: Which way?

KARAGÖZ: Just follow the moon!

The MOON appears, they fly off with her.

Night. JUNE and BAWER on the road to Dersim. They are illuminated so that they cast long shadows behind them.

Kurdish music plays softly on the car radio.

JUNE is bent over gagging into a bag.

BAWER: I can stop.

JUNE: Keep driving.

> *JUNE is still vomiting in little gasps.*

BAWER: (*Asks her in Kurdish, "How are you?"*) Çawani?

JUNE: (*Replies in Kurdish.*) Ez başim. Hewa jî gelek base. Roj baş. Cawanî. Ere. Na. Spas dikim. Hiv. Ezman. Ster Şev. Xirab.
(*I'm fine. The weather is beautiful. Hello. How are you? Yes. No. Thank you. Moon. Sky. Stars. Night. Terrible.*)

She wipes her mouth.

I've never killed anyone.

BAWER: He did though. He did. She was floating in the water. Her body was broken.

JUNE: I've never even seen a dead body before.

BAWER: That's why I came so suddenly there.

JUNE: When you took the notebook...

BAWER: He just made a move—

JUNE: My hands connected to his chest, I felt something give way. I had no other movement to make.

BAWER: You saved me. You did it by instinct.

JUNE: I always thought God was our instinct.
I don't know what God is now.

BAWER: Why did you leave your life to come here?

JUNE: I had a dream about Cem: He was here, but I could see him from my window in Nashville, he was floating in water, like you described her, floating, face down. In the water there were American flags, floating like trash. And people were watching. Nobody moved, they just left him in the water. I was screaming, I was screaming, Please somebody get him. Somebody pull him out of the water. I could see him, but I couldn't reach him. That's when I took the money from my church and fuck them. What do we do? We cry in our windows, little television windows looking at the world.

BAWER: What is this guy with his brights? The light. It's so bright. I can't see.

JUNE: Bawer, that looks like...it's getting really close...like some kind of military thing. Is that a tank?

Lights get brighter and brighter. Then to black.

Shadow Puppets:

KARAGÖZ, KOOLIOZ, HACIVAT stand on and around the police car. They are in Washington DC.

KARAGÖZ: Is this Washington DC? Is this Washington DC?

HACIVAT: Gee it's so phallic here.

KARAGÖZ: Hey, do they make democracy here?

HACIVAT: They use that beautiful big phallus over there to manufacture and export it.

KOOLIOZ: What?

KARAGÖZ: He said they use a mallet to fracture and distort it.

HACIVAT: No no no idiot EXPORT it. Right my man, Koolioz?

KOOLIOZ: Sure man..., they exporting so much, we're running out of it here...

HACIVAT: Let's take a stroll down Pennsylvania Avenue.

They bob up and down as if walking.

KARAGÖZ: Where's the White House? Where's the White House?

The White House appears on the larger screen behind them.

KOOLIOZ: There.

HACIVAT: How much do they charge to get in?

KOOLIOZ: This ain't no amusement park. It's Democracy. They don't charge for... Oh...ten dollars...

HACIVAT: Why do you want to go in there?

KARAGÖZ: Idiot! He's going to help us get our souls. He's American. They'll listen to him.

HACIVAT: Look! The American President.

The AMERICAN PRESIDENT is seen in the White House.

KOOLIOZ: I'm going to talk to him now.

KOOLIOZ disappears. Suddenly the WOLF appears with the PRESIDENT.

KARAGÖZ: OH NO! WOLF! WOLF!

HACIVAT: What's he doing here!

The WOLF and the PRESIDENT kiss each other obscenely.

KARAGÖZ / HACIVAT: Oooooo! Disgusting!

The WOLF takes a big bag labeled "souls," he lifts it up. We hear cries of hundreds of souls inside the bag.

KARAGÖZ: Our souls!

HACIVAT: He's eating them!

The PRESIDENT holds up a handful of weapons, airplanes, etc. They feed each other. The PRESIDENT feeds weapons to the WOLF, the WOLF feeds souls to the PRESIDENT. The souls cry out in falsetto voices as they are devoured.

Suddenly KOOLIOZ is seen in the White House.

KARAGÖZ: No! Koolioz.

HACIVAT: Danger.

WOLF: Black man in the White House.

A shot rings out. KOOLIOZ falls and disappears.

HACIVAT: Koolioz!

Suddenly, KARAGÖZ appears on top the White House.

KARAGÖZ: I'll save him.

The WOLF and the PRESIDENT see KARAGÖZ.

WOLF: Witness. Kill him!

HACIVAT: Run KARAGÖZ Run.

KARAGÖZ slides down into the White House.

KARAGÖZ can be seen everywhere, appearing and disappearing right behind, above and below the PRESIDENT and the WOLF. The WOLF sniffs the air. The PRESIDENT and the WOLF cross come from opposite directions trapping KARAGÖZ between them.

PRESIDENT: Terrorist!

WOLF: Terrorist!

KARAGÖZ: Swear to God I'm just a lobbyist!

The WOLF and the PRESIDENT lunge for KARAGÖZ. He ducks. The WOLF and PRESIDENT bump heads.

PRESIDENT: Misunderestimated.

HACIVAT: (*Appears:*) Stand back! I will confuse the beast with logic.

The WOLF instantly swallows HACIVAT.

KARAGÖZ: My country eats its own people!

The WOLF looms large; his shadow begins to cover KARAGÖZ.

Moon, where are you? Moon? Can you help me? You said there were laws against this Wolf.

The WOLF's shadow completely covers KARAGÖZ.

Jandarma checkpoint.

JUNE, GABE and a TURKISH GENERAL. The GENERAL sits staring, unsmiling.

GABE: Nashville. I had to pressure them a lot.
Don't show emotion.

JUNE: What happened to Bawer?

GABE: He's getting medical treatment.

JUNE: Bull crap. Where is he?

GABE: He tried to run away. He's gone.

JUNE: Gone?

GABE: They shot him.

Pause.

Think of yourself in this moment. They say you were bringing aid to the terrorists. Ten thousand dollars. They're trying to get in touch with someone from our government. They are saying the people you were with, were murdered by the PKK. Were you a hostage of the man who was driving?

JUNE: How can you work with these people?

GABE: They don't care what color my skin is. Not like in our country. The only color they care about is green. Do you want to get out of here? We can say you were a hostage who's happy to make a big donation to the army. Okay?

The GENERAL gestures "enough has been said;" stares in JUNE's eyes.

He wants me to tell you, that this is a democracy. He wants me to say, this is a beautiful country, a tolerant country. He says people come here and write lies about this country. It hurts him. He doesn't understand why. He will allow you to be taken to our corporate housing.

Later you may be called back for more questions. Is that understood?

JUNE: Okay.

GABE nods to the GENERAL. The GENERAL exits.

Can you get me to Ovacik? There's a village near there I have to get to.

Shadow Puppets:

KARAGÖZ in a small cell. Through the window of the cell we see the MOON, but it's distant, far away.

KARAGÖZ: Moon!

MOON: KARAGÖZ, what are you doing?

KARAGÖZ: They caught me. I tried to do what you said. I tried to tell them but they didn't understand...

MOON: What?

KARAGÖZ: Maybe to understand, you have to understand my language.

MOON: Teach me.

KARAGÖZ: If you can help get me out of here, I will.

Sound of bubbles. Water rising.

MOON: Just jump up!

KARAGÖZ: I can't! You have to come down.

MOON: Silly, the moon can't come down from the sky. God would be angry.

KARAGÖZ: Okay then, I'll just die.

MOON: Don't die... KARAGÖZ! KARAGÖZ!

He starts to drown. The MOON comes down and lifts him up.

KARAGÖZ: What about Hacivat and Koolioz? Can we save them too?

MOON: No. I can only save one.
Hang on, we're going to fly—let's go...

They fly away.

JUNE on the road.

A LITTLE GIRL approaches.

JUNE: Torunoba Nerede? Hello?

> *The LITTLE GIRL looks at her then runs off.*
>
> *JUNE stands looking lost. SOSIN enters.*

Torunoba nerede?

SOSIN: Torunoba?

JUNE: Yes.

SOSIN: Igilizce?

JUNE: American, from America.

SOSIN: Why are you looking for Torunoba?

JUNE: You speak English very well.

SOSIN: No. Maybe better than your Turkish. I've been working in Istanbul.

JUNE: Do you know where Torunoba is?

SOSIN: I am from Torunoba.

JUNE: Are we close? I've been walking all day. Is there a dolmus? Is there a donkey?

SOSIN: Why do you want to find Torunoba?

JUNE: I'm looking for a man named Cem Yildiz. He's from Torunoba. Do you know where that is?

SOSIN: Who are you really?

JUNE: I'm a friend. Of Cem's. Do you know him?

SOSIN: I'm Cem's sister. I'm Sosin.

> *JUNE embraces SOSIN.*

JUNE: I'm June. I think I saw pictures of you.

SOSIN: I was younger...when Cem went to America.

JUNE: Where is he?

SOSIN: Don't you know?

JUNE: I—knew that he got deported. I was hoping he would be here. He showed me so many pictures of Torunoba. The mountains. It's beautiful here.

SOSIN: This isn't Torunoba.

JUNE: But is he there? Is it close? Is he okay? I feel like he's close. It seems like he could have been standing right there just a minute ago. Like I just missed him. Can you take me to Torunoba?

SOSIN: You can't go to Torunoba now.

JUNE: Is there a military occupation?

SOSIN: Nobody can go there now.

JUNE: He's there, isn't he. I am Cem's friend. Is he hiding there? Nobody followed me here. I came alone. You can trust me.

SOSIN: It doesn't exist anymore. Because of the dam. It's all underwater. Most people went to the city. I just come back for the summer. Torunoba is gone. Everything.

JUNE: And what about Cem?

SOSIN: What was his life like in America? What kind of job did he do? Did he work? What kind of house did he live in. Did he love someone? Did he get married?

JUNE: Here.

JUNE gives SOSIN the notebook.

If you can read this, maybe this has the answer.

SOSIN reads through the book.

SOSIN: Oh... (*She reads.*)

Wexta kî ew te dixendiqînin (**When they drown you**)
Cigerên te tijî diwin av (**The water fills up your lungs**)

91

û her cihê ku bîrhatin lê jiyane tu bîr dikî tu kîyî
(*And every place where memory lived, you forget who*
you are)

When they drown you
The water fills up your lungs
And every place where memory lived
You forget who you are
But in one moment
I was thinking of fireflies
I caught one once
When I was in the village
And I was thinking how amazing
These insects have electricity
We didn't have it in the village
All the electricity sent to the west
Now they build dams on the Tigris and Euphrates
And the villages drown
The insects have electricity
We don't.

She looks at JUNE.

These are his shadow plays.

JUNE: You haven't seen him?

SOSIN: They wouldn't give us his body. They took him when
he came to the airport. Atatürk Airport. That's where they
got him. What did you think? What did you think would
happen to him? If they sent him back. Are you surprised?
You're quiet. You can't speak. It is the first time I have
ever seen an American, quiet, not talking, you usually
have so much to say. You must have cared about him a lot
to come here. You must be a good person.

She opens the book again.

Transition to last Shadow Play.

She zooms up into the sky.

We see CEM. *He is operating the puppets.*

The MOON *and* KARAGÖZ *float across the sky, past clouds.*

KARAGÖZ: It's peaceful up here.

MOON: How funny, you can speak English now Karagöz.

KARAGÖZ: Hhmf.

MOON: We can finally talk.

KARAGÖZ: But this isn't me.

MOON: We always talked. With one word or two.

KARAGÖZ: Maybe with our bodies.

The MOON *laughs.*

MOON: No!

KARAGÖZ: You're blushing.

MOON: I'm sorry. Yes.

JUNE takes the puppet from CEM. *As herself:*

JUNE: Yes.

CEM: Every language is carrying something. I've always had two people inside me, this Turkish man... I learned to become, and this Kurdish man, underneath. My first language I learned from my mother. Then I had to become, this American, but I was really myself with you.

JUNE: I knew that.

CEM: With some people you feel what's inside the language. Maybe it's something I saw in your eyes. I thought you understood me.

JUNE: But I didn't.

He gives her a puppet of herself, he operates a puppet of himself:

CEM: Some people are looking for me, immigration people. The FBI. Maybe, I think, time to go away.

JUNE: What do you mean?

CEM PUPPET: I need to get a lawyer. I need some help.

JUNE PUPPET: What did you do?

JUNE: Nothing. I know that.

JUNE PUPPET: But what did you do?

CEM: You know after 9/11 a lot of things became different for me. People looked at me with suspicion. With hate. I was from the Middle East.

JUNE PUPPET: But you have a green card.

CEM: Yes, I had one, but they have decided to contest my original application for asylum. They say they want to deport me.

JUNE PUPPET: Deport you? To where?

CEM: Back to where I came from, to my country. I lived like a guest in my own country. If they send me back I won't even be that.

JUNE PUPPET: They're not going to send you back. It's not going to happen. They made a mistake.

CEM: Canim, they can do anything they want now. A lot of people are getting disappeared.

JUNE PUPPET: What does that mean?

CEM: Simple. Take you. Put you on a plane. Send you back. Or worse.

JUNE PUPPET: That's the bad people.

CEM: Well, that would be me.

JUNE PUPPET: But you didn't do anything wrong.

CEM: Retroactively, they say I am a terrorist.

JUNE: Retroactively.

CEM: I'm dividing the state.

JUNE: But you had political asylum.

CEM: Everything I did to get political asylum is what will get me deported. They gave me a letter to go there and surrender. I never bombed anyone. I never killed anyone. I never shot a weapon.

JUNE PUPPET: Then it's just a misunderstanding. This is America, it's not like in your country. Nothing bad can happen to you, we have laws.

CEM: They are making their own laws now, they can do what they want, and they've decided I'm a terrorist.

Pause.

I love the idea of America June.
I want to be an American citizen. But right now, they say I am a terrorist. Part of a terrorist organisation.

JUNE: That's just a mistake.

CEM: What about your house?

JUNE PUPPET: What?

CEM: I need a place to hide.

JUNE PUPPET: Hide you? Do you need money? I'll help you, you can trust me, I'm your friend.

CEM: Hide me. Let me stay a few days. Then I promise, I'll go.

JUNE PUPPET: But Cem, you're a man. I can't... I'm... I want to help you, but there are other reasons.

CEM: Are you afraid of me?

JUNE: Yes, I was afraid. I was a coward.

CEM: Okay that's okay. Listen. Can you keep this for me? No matter what? It's something I wrote in my own language. I want you to have it.

JUNE: Why?

CEM: It took me a long time to write. I couldn't before, I had to study. It's important to me. I wrote it for you.

JUNE: But I can't read it.

CEM: Maybe someday you will.

JUNE: I'm sorry...

CEM: I can translate for you...are you afraid to understand it?

JUNE: No.

CEM: Are you afraid to understand what happens? What happened to me?

JUNE: Not anymore.

CEM: To be in a small room,
     Looking at the wall
     But still remembering life outside,
     Our families, or village
     Our language, our life
     Not to allow the destruction of the world
     Even if they empty our houses
     Submerge our villages
     That world is inside me
     That life is still here
     And maybe in a hundred years
     Things will be different
     These walls will get broken instead
     Walls will get broken instead of our bodies
     Walls will be broken instead of our lives.
     Do you understand?

JUNE: Yes.

Lights out.

www.ingramcontent.com/pod-product-compliance
Ingram Content Group UK Ltd.
Pitfield, Milton Keynes, MK11 3LW, UK
UKHW031252020325
455690UK00007B/85

9 781840 028423